THE
SEVEN
LAWS
and PRINCIPLES that Govern SUCCESS

By Life Coach Joe Turchi

978-1-965552-55-1 (Paperback)

BOOKWRIGHTS
HOUSE

admin@bookwrightshouse.com
☎ (213) 286 6700

Dedication

To my wife Leslie who has always been by my side in all my crazy dreams and business ventures. You have always had faith and trust in me. To my children Eric, Libbie and Taylor who I respect, love and appreciate more than they can ever know.

Foreword

Joe Turchi grew up in the traditional South Philadelphia row home, now made famous in the hit movie, *Rocky*. The neighborhood and his surroundings were exactly those depicted in the epic movie classic, and his family of twelve bonded together and survived a tough environment.

He was determined he would be one of the first in his neighborhood to go to college and use his education to rise above his humble beginnings. Well, **first goal accomplished!** Graduating from Penn State University was a milestone for Joe and the pride of the Turchi family and the South Philly neighborhood he loved.

He was a natural as a schoolteacher in the inter-city in his beloved Philadelphia. It was immediately apparent to all that he was destined to be an engaging and successful teacher and soon, a community leader. He continued his education by acquiring a master's degree at Temple University and furthered his way by acquiring leadership and administrative credentials. **Goal number two, accomplished.**

The principles that Joe has mastered, nurtured, and lives every day and is about to share with you led him to manage his own million-dollar real estate company, establish the second largest entertainment company on the East Coast with his old neighborhood friends, and raise a loving family. Twelve years as a motivational speaker helping young entrepreneurs attain their goals and dreams is his special gift.

Embracing Coach Joe and his enormous passion for helping others and his desire for you to begin your success journey is a must. Applying his proven principles in this book will be a life-changing and wondrous, rewarding journey. Please feel free to call or send an email to Coach Joe at any point of your journey as he would love to hear your success story.

I have known Joe for over twenty years, and he is a true success story and will make you one as well!

Mike Tendler
President of Lead Net Advisors, author, speaker

> *Everybody has a story to tell.*

Introduction

Chances are, if you picked up this book, you are probably like most of us looking for more out of life. Maybe you have been trying for years to find the secret to success and happiness and have not gotten the results you expected. Let's face it, there is a lot of misleading information out there, as well as get-rich-quick programs that may give you advice to achieve success without any effort. It was once said that the key to success is that successful people form habits of doing the things that are necessary to achieve success, whereas unsuccessful people refuse to perform the habits in order to achieve success. As you begin reading, the real question you must ask yourself is which person do you want to see when you look in the mirror?

Over decades of applying these seven principles, many of my clients and colleagues have experienced enormous success not only in their financial endeavors but through different areas of their life. In order for your success to begin, you must start with putting these principles into *action*.

As a coach for thirty-plus years, I have witnessed people who struggle in their pursuit of success and happiness by utilizing life's turbulent road map and heading in the wrong direction. Today is your day to command your internal GPS to *recalculate*. Although I am not a fan of the phrase "feeling stuck," I do believe we can find ourselves in a rut. I wrote this book for the reader who really wants more out of life to avoid staying in the rut. It is a book for the person who has a burning desire for success and happiness and is willing to follow this proven blueprint. It is my belief that if you read and apply these seven simple principles consistently to your daily life, success will come your way.

In the past several years of my own journey of personal growth, I spent hours on a daily basis studying the psychology of winning, success habits, and achieving happiness. What I found is that it is extremely important for us to focus on our awareness and to be totally conscious of what we truly want in life. If your present thinking is not helping you achieve your goals, it is time to change your mindset. It has often been said: "If you want to change some things in your life, you have to change the things in your life." This requires a conscious inventory check of what is working and what can you change. In essence, this is the reason I wrote this book. It is my desire to share with you these principles that have impacted my thinking, changed my mindset, and helped me achieve overall success.

Now if you have the skeptic tendencies that I possessed in my past, you may be saying, "Is this really true?" The answer is yes. "Can it work for me?" The answer is yes. Finally, if you are a procrastinator and you are thinking in your head maybe I will do this *someday*, the majority of the time, *someday* never comes.

In Napoleon Hill's famous book, *Think and Grow Rich*, he states the best antidote for procrastination is to *"DO IT NOW"*. I encourage you to take the next step on your journey to success, happiness, and becoming the leader you are meant to be by **doing it now**.

7 Laws that Transform

Here are the principles and laws that transformed my life, and I certainly believe that they will transform yours.

As a personal life coach and motivational speaker and educator for the last thirty years, I have attended many seminars throughout the United States. In my readings and extensive studying the topics of leadership, goal setting, behavior psychology, emotional intelligence, teamwork, time management, and personal growth, it has instilled in me a passion to pay these success principles forward.

I have listened to thousands of CDs (and believe it or not, cassette tapes) of many leaders and experts on the subject of success and winning. It would be impossible for me to share all of the laws and principles in this book, so I took some time to reflect back to the most powerful and impactful principles that I know transformed my life and—I am certain with application—will transform yours.

I condensed them into seven life-changing laws that will help you along on your journey.

I commend you for your desire to move closer to greatness and wish you well in your success and happiness. It is my passion to help others win in the game of life and to become lifelong learners. I look forward to hearing from you personally about the many success stories on your life's journey. Please feel free to reach out to me for more resources at J.turchi6@gmail.com or visit Inspiruslifecoaching.com

Joe Turchi

Principle #1

Definite Purpose

The Crystallization of Desire into Action

You must have a clear, compelling vision. You must have a specific aim and a clear target. To achieve this goal, you must develop a burning desire to achieve it. It needs to become an obsession. Each day when you wake up, your activities and focus must clearly be moving toward that defined objective or purpose you wish to accomplish. I refer to the focus as laserbeam focus rather than flashlight focus. I advise you not to use the "Shot Gun" approach where you try everything, hoping that if you throw enough mud on the wall, some of it will stick. Do what must be done with a specific intent in mind.

Principle #2

Establish a Specific Date

The Definition of Success = Distance x Time

For you to accomplish your particular goals in life, there must be a deadline. Included in this date or deadline, you will know exactly what you intend to give up and what sacrifices are necessary to attain your goal.

> *There is no success without sacrifice.*

Principle #3

Action Plan

You're Heading in the Wrong Direction ... But Are You Making Good Time?

Wandering around without a road map and expecting to arrive at your destination by pure luck is foolish.

There must be a written plan of action or a road map, so to speak, and you must begin ... at the beginning.

Sounds simple, so why complicate things?

Step one: Write out a clear, concise statement of what you intend to accomplish. Be precise, but do not be afraid to *think big*. Include not only financial or money goals but personal, family, and relationship goals. Also include in this exercise the things you want to do and the places you want to see. **Do not forget your spiritual goals.**

Step two: Determining what you are going to specifically do to accomplish them. Here is where the "rubber meets the road." This is the systematic, hourby-hour, day-by-day rigors of getting it to happen. This does not need to be torture; it needs to be rewarding. My advice is to treat yourself to a reward (e.g., a new tie, a new pair of shoes, or just a trip to the city, park, museum, or to see a movie) for making it happen.

You got it!

Step three: Identify the period of time to get it done. The definition of work = d x t (distance times time). Time is the element that makes it all worthwhile. Think about this: Pushing a ball up a hill in one or two hours a day defines work. Obviously, the work required to push the ball uphill is significantly different if you're doing it for one hour or an entire day. The work required to achieve any goal needs to be separated into short-term, intermediate, and long-term goals.

Step four: A developed and structured action plan means exactly what it states. What are you going to do to realize your goal? In sales, for example, how many phone calls are you going to make today? How many potential customers are you going to visit today? How many emails are you going to return today to reach new clients? In every particular sales industry, there is a number correlating to the activity you perform to the number of sales you close. This is referred to as a conversion factor. Every phase of the sales process is planned and examined for success.

When I work with some clients seeking a career change or needing a job in their field, there is always an action plan put in place. We will start with the resumé. In today's environment, resumés are critical. Employers are extremely busy and do not want to spend a lot of time figuring out your skill set. It needs to be concise, and you must highlight yourself clearly and quickly. Resumés take some time to create, but they are worth it. As a team, my clients and I set up a personal networking plan of action, an internet plan of action, and a cold call plan of action with resumés in hand. On my website Inspiruslifecoaching.com you will see an animation of how this whole process works. In career coaching, we develop a thirty-day plan of action with four steps:

PLAN DO CHECK ADJUST

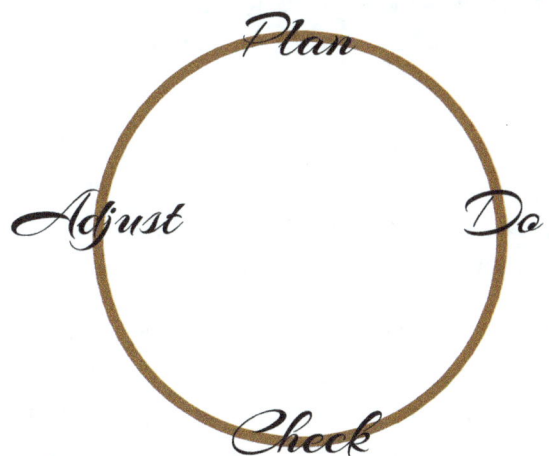

Principle #4

Affirm Your Action Plan Daily

The Person Who Can't Manage Their Time Can't Manage an Outcome!

The statistics and facts make it clear: Goals are rarely accomplished without being written out to read and affirm every day.

Each day when you begin your day, read aloud your definite purpose action plan. As you retire for the evening, once more you should affirm your goal by reading it aloud. (It sounds silly, but it works.)

These actions reinforce your vision and your belief system to assure your subconscious mind that you will achieve your dreams and goals. It tells your brain that it is possible. It affirms a clear, compelling vision.

This I refer to as "Possibility Thinking."

> ***Goals will never be achieved without writing them down.***

Principle #5

PMA (Positive Mental Attitude)

> **Attitude is everything!**

With this statement, some people always share with me that they have a good attitude, but it doesn't always work. Then, when I spend more time with them, they realize they do not apply or execute the PMA concept. They may be talking the talk, but not walking the walk. We are surrounded by a negative environment everywhere we go work, home, traffic, church, department stores, service industry, etc. Most of your day, you are surrounded by people constantly complaining. This can be contagious. Have you ever noticed those people who come toward you, and you just want to avoid them because of their negativity?

I highly recommend Dale Carnegie's book, *How to Win Friends and Influence People*. In one of his chapters, he says we should never *criticize, condemn, or complain*. It is a motto that we all should practice. One of the best attitude quotes that I absolutely love was written by Charles Swindoll:

"The longer I live, the more I realize the impact of attitude on life. Attitude, to me, is more important than facts. It is more important than the past, than education, than money, than circumstances, than failure, than successes, than what other people think or say or do. It is more important than appearance, giftedness or skill. It will make or break a company...a church...a home.

"The remarkable thing is we have a choice every day regarding the attitude we will embrace for that day. We cannot change our past...we cannot change the fact that people will act in a certain way. We cannot change the inevitable. The only thing we can do is play on the one string we have, and that is our attitude.

"I am convinced that life is 10% what happens to me and 90% of how I react to it. And so it is with you...we are in charge of our attitudes."

—*Charles Swindoll*

With many of the people that I coach, I give them this quote, and I ask them to put this in a place that they can read it twice per day. What a transformation this has over people. When I meet people all over the country, I share with them my daily mantra: *Monday is Marvelous, Tuesday is Terrific, Wednesday is Wonderful, Thursday is Tremendous, Friday is Fantastic, Saturday is Super, and Sunday is Stupendous.* If you are reading this right now, you might be saying to yourself, "This guy does not know my situation." Well, it is my belief that any situation is changeable. It is important to realize that you can practice habits that will improve any situation as well as your attitude.

Here are some tips as to how you can change your life for the better forever:

First, you must believe in yourself.

> *When you believe in yourself, you are forced to focus on ways to improve yourself and reach for your full potential.*

Second, you must have a willingness to see the best in others.

> *Each day, go through life catching everyone you see doing something good and edify them on their goodness.*

Third, always develop the habits of seeing opportunity everywhere.

> *When the opportunity hits you in the face, seize the moment and go for it... Do not procrastinate.*

Fourth, focus on solutions and ask the right questions.

Over the years with my experience in coaching, I have developed a simple formula for solving any challenge in life. If you truly take the time to apply this formula, I promise you it will work. Simply take a piece of paper and write down these four questions and your answers. Your solution will appear.

> *What is the problem?*
>
> *What is the cause of the problem?*
>
> *What are the possible solutions to the problem?*
>
> *What is the best solution to do now?*

I admit this is simple common sense, but this exercise produces results that you cannot imagine. Try it and have fun with it.

Fifth, create a desire within to be a giver.

> *Giving is the highest level of living.*
> *Always add value to people you meet and those you spend time with.*

Sixth, be persistent.

> *Winners never quit. Quitters never win.*

Seventh, take responsibility for your life.

> *Don't blame the ball for losing the game.*

Always be willing to look in the mirror, be accountable for your actions, and move forward with personal responsibility.

Principle #6

Thinking for a Change

It has been said that thoughts are things. Good or bad, you become what you think about every day. Earl Nightingale recorded a speech in the 1950s called "The Strangest Secret." (If you can download this, do it now!) He attributed the lack of success to us as human beings not taking the time to THINK on a regular basis. I know this is so true for many people I meet. As we exist in society today, we form the habit of going to work and then traveling home, never really taking the time to truly stop and think. We create the routine of home to work to sleep, and then wake up the next day and continue the same habit. Albert Einstein once said,

> *"The height of insanity is doing the same thing over and over again and expecting different results."*

To look at this at another level, think of it as the law of attraction. What you focus on in your mind is what you attract. If you focus on losing your home or never having any money or not even feeling good about yourself, it is bound to happen. If you picture good thoughts, you will eventually get those things. This is very simple to practice. When you affirm every day what you will accomplish, you will get what you picture!

Principle #7

Leaders Are Readers

On my travels during my public-speaking seminars, I had the privilege of meeting two great gentlemen, Chad Connelly, a business partner from South Carolina, and Charlie "Tremendous" Jones. Charlie was an incredible top fifty round-table speaker who owned a book publishing company in Mechanicsburg, PA. Charlie spent most of his life educating millions of people on how important reading can be for their personal development. His famous quote that I carry with me always is:

> **"Five years from now the person you will become will be based on the books you read and the people you associate with."**

I feel honored to have had both Chad and Charlie as mentors and as friends, and I will always cherish their teaching moments. I feel as though I would leave you uninformed if at this time I did not share with you the most influential books that took me from mediocrity to excellence.

- *Think and Grow Rich* by Napoleon Hill
- *How to Win Friends and Influence People* by Dale Carnegie
- *The Magic of Thinking Big* by David Swartz
- *The Power of Focus* by Jack Canfield
- *The Magic of Believing* by Claude Bristol
- *7 Habits of Highly Successful People* by Stephen Covey
- *Rich Dad Poor Dad* by Robert Kiyosaki
- *How I Raised Myself from Failure to Success in Selling* by Frank Bettger
- *21 Irrefutable Laws of Leadership* by John Maxwell
- *Freedom Tide* by Chad Connelly
- *How to Have Power and Confidence with People* by Les Giblin
- *The Power of Intention* by Wayne Dyer
- *Life Is Tremendous* by Charlie "Tremendous" Jones
- *Psycho-Cybernetics* by Maxwell Maltz And last but not least,
- *The Maxwell Leadership Bible* by John Maxwell

When I am asked to speak to any particular group on goal setting, I always begin with the explanation that goals rarely will ever be accomplished without writing them down and associating a deadline for them to be completed. This helps to create a vision as to when your goals will become a reality.

The illustration or formula I often teach is based on four concepts:

The Bridge of Success

Self-improvement means getting from Point A to Point B, or from one side of the bridge to the other.

It's all about **BE — DO — HAVE.**

Consciously, or subconsciously, we all want to ...

BE someone, **DO** something, or **HAVE** something in life.

The dream is the thought! The dream only becomes a goal when you, in fact, identify a date you expect to accomplish the goal. Simply put, a *dream* becomes a *goal* when you put a deadline on it.

> ***A dream is a progressive realization of a worthwhile goal with a timeframe.***

However, for anyone to get to their goal, I encourage and teach that you must cross over a "bridge" on your journey from your dream to your goal! This bridge is not constructed with steel or iron but with conviction, with vision, and with a belief that you can achieve the goal. To cross the bridge, you must have the determination and commitment to do so! See it, and you will achieve it! With understanding that your thoughts have divine powers and will manifest themselves positively or negatively, it is totally up to you!

Here is a true story of the power of "Seeing is believing." I was working with a young man named Eric with big dreams and an effervescing personality you just wanted to be around. In our preliminary interview and coaching sessions, I asked him what he hoped to accomplish from our sessions together. I was astounded when I heard his vision and what I heard next. "A boat captain." "That is awesome!" I replied.

"Nevertheless," I thought to myself, "how can I help him cross the bridge for such an audacious dream?" I had my work cut out for me! So to crystallize the dream, I took him to a marina where he could smell the sea, hear the gulls, see the sun sparkle on the waves, and admire the twenty-five-foot, thirtyfive-foot, fifty-five-foot yachts. I asked him the key question, "Which one of these babies would you like to be the captain of?"

His eyes grew wider, and he pointed to the fifty-fivefoot yacht. It allowed him to dream big and visualize himself in the fifty-five-foot yacht. At that point, he did more than just believe that he could actually accomplish his dream; he visualized himself in that boat, felt the wheel in his hand, saw the horizon at sunset and sunrise, and adjusted for the constant rocking beneath his feet.

This is where there must be commitment, and reality must set in. The next step in the formula, *commitment,* is critical. Eric needed to focus on the credentials to qualify to be a professional captain on his fifty-fivefoot yacht. A large and daunting task. We decided that the education and curriculum needed was to search out maritime schools. He chose a school in Maine: Maine Maritime Academy. He spent years of study, commitment, and hard work. The visualization from that day at the marina was constantly clear in his mind. After all his effort, the formula worked. Eric today, at twenty-five years old, is navigating 270- and 370-foot ships in the Gulf of Mexico, servicing oil rigs for a huge shipping company.

WINNING STARTS WITH BEGINNING!

I hope this information is helpful for you to *think big* and chase your dreams.

I would love your feedback as well as to hear your new story and how this book impacted your life.

Please send any information to …

J.turchi6@gmail.com

Acknowledgements

I would especially like to thank, Julia Ripa for helping me get started with the manuscript process, you are an awesome person! Thank you to Kathy Vieldhouse for picking up the pieces when it was time to wrap up the final product, you are special in my heart. Thank you, to my daughter Elizabeth for guiding me during the manuscript startup process. Lastly Thank you to my daughter Taylor, who has been incredibly patient and inspiring. I am so proud to have you as my daughter, keep charging my tenacious Pitbull.